BIG CATS

The Natural History Museum Library

BIG CATS

A selection of magnificent illustrations by
JOSEPH WOLF
first published in London in 1883

Wordsworth Editions

This edition published 1991 by Wordsworth Editions Ltd,
8b East Street, Ware, Hertfordshire,
in association with the Natural History Museum, London.

Copyright © Wordsworth Editions Ltd 1991.

All rights reserved. This publication may not be
reproduced, stored in a retrieval system,
or transmitted, in any form or by any means, electronic,
mechanical, photocopying, recording or otherwise,
without the prior permission of the publishers.

ISBN 1-85326-963-8

Printed and bound in Hong Kong by South China Printing Co.

Acknowledgements

The publishers would like to thank the many people at the Natural History Museum, London, who made publication of this book possible; in particular Daphne Hills, Zoology Department, Rex Banks, Head of Library Services, Librarians Anne Datta and Carol Gokce, together with Tim Parmenter and his staff in the Photographic Department.

Introduction

THE ILLUSTRATIONS of the great cats of the world in this book come from one of the most beautiful works ever produced on the subject. Entitled *A Monograph of the Felidae or the Family of Cats*, it represents a combination of the talents of two remarkable men, Daniel Giraud Elliot and Joseph Wolf.

Wolf's generous patron, D.G. Elliot (1835-1915), the author and originator of the work, was born in New York City of wealthy parents. In the fashion of the times, his health was thought to be too delicate to allow of his going to college, and instead he was sent abroad to enjoy the grandest of Grand Tours. He travelled extensively in Europe, Egypt, Turkey, the West Indies and Brazil, and during this time he acquired an astonishing collection of bird and animal skins, though birds were his first love. Because of this, he came to follow the lead of the English 'bird man' John Gould in publishing large folio ornithologies, including works on thrushes, hornbills, pheasants and birds of paradise. He was an accomplished artist, and some of these monographs were illustrated from his own brush, but for others he employed the services of some of the greatest wildlife artists of his day such as Wolf and John Gerard Kaulemans. He spent ten years from 1869 in London, then the centre of natural history studies, and his scholarship so impressed the Zoological Society of London that he was elected a Fellow of the Society. During his time in London his interest in mammals grew, and it was in this period that the work was done which culminated in *Felidae* published in 1883. On his return to America, he was instrumental in founding the American Onithologists Union, and was its second President from 1890-1891. In 1894, the year following the great Chicago exhibition, he was appointed Curator of Zoology at the Chicago Museum of Natural History until his retirement in 1906. Even then he was not idle, and in 1912, at the age of 77, he published his *Review of Primates*. After his death in 1915 the National Academy of Sciences established the Elliot Medal for meritorious publications in zoology.

Joseph Wolf (1820-1899), the illustrator of *Felidae*, was born in Germany of prosperous farming stock. His love of nature and his artistic ability were apparent at an early age, and at sixteen he was apprenticed to Gebruder Becker in Koblenz, a leading lithography firm. This experience of working on stone was invaluable for his later work in book illustration. After some years in Leiden and Darmstadt he was engaged to produce illustrations for Schlegel and

Wulverhort's great *Traité de Fauconnerie*. The 'year of revolutions', 1848, inclined him to feel that Britain might be a more stable base from which to develop his career, and in that year he moved to London. His work was appreciated straight away, and in 1849 he exhibited his picture *Woodcocks Seeking Shelter* at the Royal Academy. He was also commissioned to illustrate Grey's *Genera of Birds* and was taken up by John Gould, which gave him access to the Zoological Society of London. There he added to his already considerable reputation by providing a series of remarkable illustrations for both the Proceedings and the Transactions of the Society. At the same time, he was employed by Gould (whom he seems to have disliked as heartily as did Edward Lear) to work on *Birds of Great Britain*. By the time that Elliot came to London, Wolf was ready to work with a more congenial collaborator, and the monographs on *Phasaniadae* and *Felidae* resulted. At this time he was also illustrating Dresser's *Birds of Europe*. After Elliot's return to the United States, Wolf remained prolific and in demand, and in 1878 he moved to Primrose Hill Studios so that he could spend more time at the zoo drawing the animals he loved.

The illustrations of *Felidae* are remarkable considering the difficulties under which Elliot and Wolf worked. Frequently, they had only one skin of dubious provenance sent from afar, and this caused some confusion. On occasion, Elliot would misattribute species because he did not realise that the differences in colouring and marking of skins were caused by animals of the same species inhabiting the extremes of their range. However, Wolf's illustrations are of a very high order, and it is difficult to disagree with Sir Edwin Landseer, who said of Wolf 'without exception, the best all-round animal painter that ever lived'.

Contents

An index by common name appears on the following leaf.

Alphabetical Index
by common name

Cheetah

Acinonyx jubatus

THE CHEETAH was formerly widely distributed across Africa and western Asia, including North Africa, rocky mid-Saharan massifs and desert fringes, as well as the plains and savanna areas south of the Sahara, Arabia, Iran Turkestan, Pakistan and north India. It still survives in a few areas in east and south-west Africa but is increasingly rare, and is now extinct in India; but a few Asian cheetah may still survive in Iran and Russian Turkestan.

The cheetah's method of hunting differs from other large cats in that it runs down its prey, usually gazelle or hares, from some distance, rather than pouncing from ambush. It is the swiftest of all quadrupeds and can achieve bursts of up to 60mph (95kph) over short distances. It is an animal designed for speed, lightly built, long legged and with narrow, almost dog-like feet, the claws of which, unlike those of most cats, cannot be fully retracted. The coat is tawny, covered with numerous closely-spaced solid spots. Head and body 1120-1500mm (44-60″); tail 600-800mm (24-32″); shoulder height 800-940mm (30-37″); weight 35-65kg (75-140lb).

Cheetahs are easy to tame; in Asia they have been used for centuries for hunting game, most recently in India where animals were even imported from Africa as the native populations became rare, and it is sometimes referred to as the hunting leopard because of this practice. The name cheetah is derived from the Hindi word *chita*, which itself comes from a Sanskrit root meaning 'speckled'.

The painting shows a female cheetah with young, tiny cubs. They are usually secreted in a thicket or long grass while their mother hunts, and have a curious mantle of long hair which is lost as they become more independent, revealing the characteristic spots.

CYNAILURUS JUBATA.

J Wolf & J Smit, del et lith.   M & N Hanhart imp.

African Golden Cat
Felis aurata

A CLOSE RELATIVE of the Asian golden cat occupying similar tropical forest habitat in Africa: deciduous woodland, thick bush and savannah edges of southern West Africa from Gambia to Cameroon, through the equatorial forests of Zaire to the mountain forests and bamboo groves of Uganda and western Kenya at heights of up to 3500m (12,000ft). A nocturnal predator, which hunts mainly on the ground but also climbs readily; favoured prey are birds, hyrax, and small antelope such as duiker. Moderate size with a relatively small head and rounded ears. Head and body 700-950mm (27-37"); tail 280-370mm (11-14"); weight 13-18kg (30-40lb).

Coat short and variable in colour from chestnut, tawny brown or fawn to bluish-grey. Some specimens, particularly those from the forests of West Africa, exhibit numerous dark spots; others are only spotted on their undersides. The depicted animals show a few of the variations which occur.

J.Wolf & J.Smit.del.et lith.

M & N Hanhart. imp.

FELIS CHRYSOTHRIX.

Bay Cat
Felis badia

A SMALLER RELATIVE of the Asiatic golden cat, the bay cat is found only on the island of Borneo. It has been rarely observed but is known to inhabit the more remote forest, scrub and rocky limestone areas. Likely prey items are birds, rodents and probably small deer. Size approximately 650mm (26″) head and body length, with a 400mm (16″) tail. Two different colour varieties have been recorded: bright chestnut as the name implies, and also a dark grey form with reddish flanks and paler underparts; the fur is short and close.

J.Wolf & J.Smit.del.et.lith.

M&N.Hanhart.imp.

FELIS BADIA.

Leopard Cat
Felis bengalensis

ONE OF THE MOST widely distributed Asian small cats ranging from North India and Nepal across China as far as the Amur River basin in Siberia and south through Indo-China, Malaysia, Indonesia to the Philippine Islands. The leopard cat prefers forested areas but can adapt to a wide variety of habitats and is even to be found near human settlements. It is an excellent swimmer and has colonised many small offshore islands. Prey includes fish as well as birds, reptiles, rodents, hares and young deer.

There is considerable variation in appearance depending on locality but the typical form has a coat of tawny or buff fur strikingly marked with large dark brown spots. Animals from the colder areas in the north of the range are larger, thicker haired, greyish in colour with rather indistinct rufous markings, while examples from the Indonesian islands are small, short haired and marked with numerous small spots. Head and body size 350-600mm (14-24″); tail 150-400mm (6-15″) weight 3-7kg (6-15lb).

The plate opposite is *Felis bengalensis*. The following pages illustrate other varieties of the Leopard Cat mistakenly entitled by Elliot and Wolf *Felis scripta*, *Felis euptilura* and *Felis javanensis*.

J.Wolf & J.Smit del. et lith.

M. & N. Hanhart imp.

FELIS BENGALENSIS.

Leopard Cat
Felis scripta

THIS LEOPARD CAT comes from Szechuan in central China. For a full description of this adaptable and widely spread animal see under *Felis bengalensis* on the previous page.

J.Wolf & J.Smit del. et lith.

M&N.Hanhart imp.

FELIS SCRIPTA.

Leopard Cat
Felis euptilura

SHOWN HERE are two leopard cats from Siberia and northern China. As with their cousins on the previous and following pages, there is a full description of them and their habit under *Felis bengalensis* on page 18.

J. Wolf & J. Smit. del. et lith.

M & N Hanhart. imp.

FELIS EUPTILURA.

Leopard Cat
Felis javanensis

THREE LEOPARD CATS from, on the left, southern China, on the right, Sumatra, and above, from Java. For a description of the leopard cat and its wide variety of distribution and habitat, see under *F. bengalensis* on page 18.

J.Wolf & J.Smit, del et lith.

M & N Hanhart imp.

1 *var.* F. CHINENSIS.

2 *var.* F. SUMATRANA.

FELIS JAVANENSIS.

Caracal

Felis caracal

THE CARACAL is a distinctive reddish-brown, lynx-like cat with long legs and large black-tufted ears, and is sometimes referred to as the Persian lynx. It is a native of both Asia and Africa, inhabiting savanna grassland and semi-desert throughout much of Africa, Arabia and the Near East, as well as southern Turkey, Iran and Turkestan to north-western India. In the past caracals were kept in captivity by Indian potentates and trained to hunt in packs for small game such as peafowl and hares. They are now on the decline in India and are absent from several former areas of distribution, but in South Africa they still occur in sufficient numbers to be considered a pest. Caracal will take small domestic livestock but their natural prey are rodents, ground nesting birds and young antelope or deer.

Head and body 550-750mm (22-30″); tail short, about 230mm (9″); weight 16-23kg (35-50lb).

J.Wolf & J.Smit del. & lith.

M & N Hanhart, imp.

FELIS CARACAL.

Jungle Cat

Felis chaus

A MEDIUM-SIZED CAT, quite long-legged with a comparatively short tail. Head and body length 600-750mm (24-30"); tail 250-350mm (10-14"); weight up to 14kg (30lb). Usually plain coloured, light brown or grey with a few obscure dark stripes on the legs and tail; the ears are prominent with small tufts.

Also known as the marsh cat, this species prefers reedbeds, marshy areas, and river banks, but also occurs in woodland and open country. It is a bold species which can sometimes be found close to human settlements hunting in village fields, particularly in the morning and at evening time. Prey includes hares, rodents, snakes and frogs and it will also feed on carrion. It ranges from Egypt eastwards through the Middle East to India, Indo-China and Sri Lanka.

J.Smit. del. et lth. M & N Hanhart. in

FELIS CHAUS.

Pampas Cat

Felis colocolo

THE PAMPAS CAT inhabits open grasslands, scrub and mountainous areas in South America from Ecuador south and east to Chile and Patagonia. The scientific name *pajeros* used by Elliot comes from the Spanish for straw because these cats often live in reed-beds. Favoured prey are small mammals such as cavies, but also birds and reptiles.

Roughly the same size as a domestic cat: head and body 520-700mm (20-27″); tail 270-330mm (10-13″); weight 3.5-6.6kg (7-13lb). Pampas cats have long lax fur, the coat is predominantly grey shading to red and sometimes spotted, particularly on the undersides; markings and coat length vary according to locality. The individual in the foreground of the painting with russet spots on the underparts is from Chile, while that standing behind has darker spotting and is the form found in Ecuador.

J. Wolf. & J. Smit. del. et. lith.

M & N Hanhart imp.

FELIS PAJEROS.

Puma

Felis concolor

THE LARGEST of the 'smaller' cats included in the genus *Felis*, also known variously as the cougar, mountain lion, panther and American lion. Formerly ranged throughout the Americas from British Columbia in Canada south through the U.S.A. to Tierra del Fuego, the southernmost tip of South America. Occupies many types of habitat: deciduous, coniferous and tropical forest, scrub, steppe grassland, semi-desert and rocky areas. Pumas have often been considered to be a threat to livestock, which has led to their virtual elimination from most of their former territory in eastern North America.

It is a solitary and secretive cat, hunting by day or night, the principal prey being deer but smaller animals are also taken. The coat is plain tawny, buff or brown and sometimes grey; the young, usually two to four in number, are spotted from birth but lose their markings when about six months of age.

Head and body 1200-1960mm (4-6ft); tail 670-780mm (2-2.5ft); weight 36-100kg (80-200lb).

J. Wolf. & J. Smit. del. et. lith.

FELIS CONCOLOR.

M & N Hanhart. imp.

Geoffroy's Cat

Felis geoffroyi

GEOFFROY'S CAT is another of the South American spotted cats but one particularly well suited to temperate climates; it inhabits scrubby woodland, open brush and rocky areas from Bolivia to Patagonia. It is a good climber and sometimes sleeps in trees; it feeds on a variety of small mammals and birds. The coat varies from light ochre to silvery grey and is covered with numerous small discrete spots.

Head and body 450-700mm (17-27"); tail 260-350mm (10-14").

The lower individual in this painting is believed to be based on the skin of an Oncilla or tiger cat, *F. tigrina*. This small cat from Central and South America is principally a forest species living on insects, lizards, birds and small rodents. The coat is of moderate length, and usually tawny with dark brown spots and rings, although black individuals also occur. The oncilla is sometimes confused with the margay because of the similarity of the markings but it does not grow as large and has a comparatively shorter tail. Head and body 400-550mm (16-21"); tail 250-400mm (10-16"); weight 3kg (6lb).

J. Wolf & J. Smit del et lith.

M & N Hanhart. imp.

FELIS GEOFFROYI.

Andean Cat

Felis jacobita

THIS PAINTING was based on an illustration and description of a specimen held in the Milan Museum, the first known example of this rare and elusive South American cat. The Andean cat inhabits the rocky slopes and arid grasslands of the Andes Mountains at heights of up to 5,000m (15,000ft), from Peru to Chile and Argentina. It is a little larger than a domestic cat – head and body 650mm (26″); tail 400mm (16″) – and has a dense coat of soft greyish fur. The principal prey are small mammals such as chinchillas, degus and other alpine rodents.

Virtually nothing is known about the habits of this cat, which has rarely been seen in the wild.

J.Wolf & J.Smit del. et lith

jachita

Hanhart imp

FELIS COLOCOLLA.

Canadian Lynx

Felis (Lynx) canadensis

A CLOSE RELATIVE of the Eurasian Lynx inhabiting the forested regions of Canada, Alaska and the northern Rocky Mountains. They feed on rodents and gamebirds and will take prey as large as deer but in the most northerly regions are largely dependent on the snowshoe hare. Crashes in the hare population are reflected in the number of lynx able to survive in the same area.

Canadian lynx have thick, light brown to greyish fur with a variable amount of indistinct spotting mainly on the under-sides; they have a large facial ruff, tufted ears, long legs and very large spreading feet which help them move through deep drifts of snow.

Head and body 840-1000mm (33-39″); tail 50-140mm (2-6″); weight 5-18kg (11-40lb).

FELIS CANADENSIS.

J.Wolf, & J.Smit, del. et lith.

M & N Hanhart. imp.

Eurasian Lynx

Felis (Lynx) lynx

THE LYNX is one of the major predators of the colder regions of Europe and Asia, feeding on deer, hares and rabbits. They inhabit coniferous forests from Scandinavia and Eastern Europe across Siberia to northern China, and are also found in Tibet and the mountains of Central Asia.

There are more isolated populations in the Iberian Peninsula, Greece, The Balkans, Turkey, northern Iran and the Caucasus; there have also been attempted re-introductions to the Alps in Central Europe.

General colouration is light or reddish brown, often with a frosting of white hairs particularly in the winter coat. The coat may be spotted although this is variable; animals from the southern parts of the range are particularly heavily marked, often more brightly coloured, and smaller. Head and body 670-1100mm (26-43″); tail very short 60-170mm (3-7″); weight 5-25kg (10-55lb).

This illustration shows a lynx from Eastern Siberia, *Felix cervaria*, a race noted for its large size.

J. Wolf & J. Smit del et lith.

M & N Hanhart imp

FELIS CERVARIA.

Eurasian Lynx

Felis (Lynx) lynx

THE SPANISH LYNX *Felis (Lynx) lynx pardina* is sometimes classified as a separate species. It is a heavily spotted form which once occurred throughout the Iberian Peninsula, now rare and restricted to a few scattered mountainous areas and the scrubland and thickets of the Guadalquivir Delta.

FELIS PARDINA.

el.et lith

M & N.Hanhart im

Bobcat

Felis (Lynx) rufus

THE BOBCAT is also known as the bay lynx. It lives in woods, thickets, rocky areas, semi-desert and swamps, and formerly occurred throughout most of the U.S.A. and Mexico, replacing the Canadian lynx in the more southerly latitudes of North America. Called here by Wolf *Felis rufa*, the bobcat closely resembles the lynx but has a redder coat, is more heavily spotted and has smaller ear-tufts. Size similar: head and body 620-900mm (24-35″); tail 120-170mm (5-7″); weight 4-18kg (10-40lb). The bobcat has a reputation for taking poultry and other small livestock which has made it a target for farmers throughout its range, but the principal natural prey are rabbits, as well as small rodents and birds.

FELIS RUFA.

J. Wolf & J. Smit del. et lith.

M & N Hanhart imp.

Pallas's Cat
Felis manul

THIS CURIOUS-LOOKING CAT inhabits the steppes, arid country, and high rocky plateaux of Central Asia, living at elevations of up to 4000m. It has very small ears, short legs and tail, and a dense coat with thick woolly underfur, adaptations to the harsh climate. The hairs on the underside are particularly long, providing good insulation for this animal which spends much of its time lying on frozen ground or snow. The coat colour varies from light grey to buff or russet. Head and body 500-650mm (20-25″); tail 210-300mm (8-12″); weight 3-5kg (6-10lb).

Pallas's cat gives birth to five to six young using a den under rocks, in a cave or in a burrow dug by other animals. It hunts mainly at night feeding on small mammals.

J.Wolf del. J.Smit lith.

M & N.Hanhart imp.

FELIS MANUL.

Marbled Cat

Felis marmorata

AN INHABITANT of forested areas of Asia from Nepal through Indo-China to Malaya, Sumatra and Borneo, but considered rare throughout most of its range. It is mainly nocturnal and arboreal, taking a variety of prey including invertebrates, snakes and lizards as well as rats, squirrels and birds. The marbled cat resembles the clouded leopard in colouration and markings but is considerably smaller. It has a coat of dense fluffy fur, rounded ears and a tail almost as long as its body. Total length about 1000mm (36″); weight up to 5kg (10lb).

Wolf & J.Smit, del. et lith.

M.& N.Hanhart imp.

FELIS MARMORATA.

Ocelot
Felis pardalis

A MEDIUM-SIZED CAT from tropical America. Head and body length 650-970mm (26-38″); tail 270-400mm (11-16″); shoulder height about 410mm (16″); weight 11-16kg (25-35lb). They have been recorded as far north as Arizona and Texas in the U.S.A. while the southern limit of the range is northern Argentina. The short-haired coat is dramatically marked with dark spots and rings, coalesced into longitudinal stripes. Ground colour varies from grey to tawny yellow, the animals with the brightest coats and the most striking markings usually living in forest, while those inhabiting scrub and semi desert areas tend to more sober hues. The animals in the foreground of the painting are from Guyana and Brazil respectively, while the individual climbing the tree behind them is from Mexico.

Ocelots hunt mainly on the ground, but also climb and swim well. They prey on birds, snakes, cavies, monkeys, and peccaries. The female usually gives birth to twins. These attractive animals used to be widely hunted for their skins, but changed attitudes to conservation and new legal restrictions have reduced this activity to some extent.

STRIPED *var:*

var: F. MELANURA.

var: F. GRISEA.

F. PARDALIS, *typical style.*

FELIS PARDALIS.

J.Wolf & J. Smit del. et lith.

M & N. Hanhart imp.

Flat-headed Cat
Felis planiceps

A RARE and secretive nocturnal cat found in southern Thailand, Malaya, Sumatra and Borneo, usually recorded from localities close to rivers and streams. The flat-headed cat has a dense coat of dark brown fur, each hair tipped with white, the eyes are close-set, while the small rounded ears are set low on the side of the head. The body appears long because of the relatively short legs and tail. Head and body length 410-500mm (16-20″); tail 130-150mm (5-6″). This cat possesses a further unusual feature in that the claws cannot be fully retracted, a condition shared by the fishing cat, which may relate to the semi-aquatic habits of both these species. The preferred prey items are fish and frogs.

J.Wolf & J.Smit. del et lith.

M.& N.Hanhart. imp.

FELIS PLANICEPS.

Rusty-spotted Cat
Felis rubiginosa

ONE OF THE SMALLEST species of the wild felids, this animal is 350–480mm (14–19″) long, with a 150–250mm (6–10″) tail and weighs 1–2kg (2–4lb). The coat is predominantly grey tinged with rusty red and marked with indistinct dark brown or russet-coloured spots and lines. Rusty-spotted cats are found only in Sri Lanka and few localities in peninsular India, principally the south-west where it inhabits mainly scrub, dry grassland and open country. In Sri Lanka it may also be found in humid, mountainous forest. It is a nocturnal hunter, preying on birds and small mammals.

FELIS RUBIGINOSA.

J.Wolf & J.Smit. del et lith.

M & N.Hanhart. imp.

Serval

Felis serval

THIS medium-sized cat is to be found in savanna areas throughout Africa south of the Sahara and also in a few localities in North Africa. Preferred habitats are scrub or grassland, often close to water; they avoid desert and equatorial forest. Favoured prey are ground nesting birds, but also insects, lizards, rodents, hares and even young antelope. The serval is extremely swift and agile, leaping as much as six feet (1.8m) in the air to catch birds which it has flushed from the undergrowth.

It is a lightly-built cat with a short tail and very long legs, a small head set on a long neck, large eyes and prominent ears; all adaptations to hunting in tall grass.

Head and body 700-1000mm (27-39″); tail about 300mm (12″). The coat is yellow ochre most commonly covered with solid black spots and bars, but a few individuals sometimes referred to as servalines have a pattern of more numerous, tiny dark sports.

Wolf. & J. Smit, del. et lith.   M & N Hanhart imp.

FELIS SERVAL

Wild Cat

Felis silvestris

THIS WIDE-RANGING cat was once to be found in suitable habitats from Great Britain across Europe, the Near and Middle East, Central Asia into north and central India and much of Africa. It has now disappeared from the more heavily populated areas of central Europe; in Britain it still survives in the Scottish Highlands. Wild cats can exist in a wide range of habitats and climates: forest, open woodland, scrub, moorland, steppe, savanna and rocky arid country. It is mainly nocturnal, hiding by day in dens under rocks or in hollow trees. Litters generally contain two to five kittens. Prey includes hares and rabbits, small rodents and ground nesting birds. The wild cat is generally a little larger than a domestic cat, light brown or grey, marked with darker stripes or spots. The size of the individuals, length and thickness of coat and type and intensity of markings, varies according to locality. Head and body 500-800mm (20-31″); tail 280-350mm (11-14″); Weight 3-6kg (6-12lb).

The examples opposite are European wild cats, *Felis silvestris silvestris*. These thick-set animals have short blunt black-tipped tails and are strongly marked with dark stripes. The Latin name *Felis catus* used by Elliot is now more usually applied to the domestic cat. House cats are descended from the African form of wild cat, and will readily interbreed with any race.

Wolf. & J.Smit, del. et lith.

Hanhart imp.

FELIS CATUS.

Wild Cat
Felis silvestris lybica

THIS AFRICAN WILD CAT, called here by Wolf *Felis caffra*, is relatively long-legged and lightly built with short fur and less distinct striping. Animals of this race tamed in Ancient Egypt became the ancestors of the domestic cat. See also under *Felis silvestris* on the previous page.

J.Wolf & J.Smit.del.et lith.

M&N.Hanhart. imp.

FELIS CAFFRA.

Wild Cat

Felis silvestris ornata

THIS is the Indian desert cat, a small distinctively spotted race of wild cat found in scrub, dry woodland and desert areas in north India and Pakistan. See also page 58.

J.Wolf.&.J.Smit.del.et.lith.

M&N.Hanhart.imp.

FELIS ORNATA.

Wild Cat
Felis silvestris caudata

T HE ILLUSTRATION HERE is an example of the wild cat from Russian Turkestan. Central Asian animals are large and thickly haired to cope with the harsh climate, and the spots are less distinct than those of the Indian form. See the main entry on wild cats on page 58.

J.Wolf & J.Smit del et lith.

M & N Hanhart imp.

FELIS CAUDATUS.

Wild Cat

Felis shawiana

THIS illustration is based on a specimen obtained in Yarkand in Chinese Turkestan and named *F. shawiana* after the collector. There has been some doubt about its actual identity but the skin is now usually accepted to be an example of Turkestan wild cat. See the main entry on wild cats on page 58.

J. Wolf. & J. Smit, del & lith.

Hanhart imp

FELIS SHAWIANA.

Asiatic Golden Cat

Felis temminckii

WIDELY but sparsely distributed across South East Asia from Nepal and Burma east to China and south through Indo-China to Malaya and Sumatra, this cat's preferred habitats are deciduous and tropical forest but it will also occupy more open terrain. It feeds on game birds, rodents, hares and small deer but will sometimes prey on goats and other small domestic livestock.

Felis temminckii is a medium-sized cat with a head and body length of 750-1020mm (30-40″), tail 400-550mm (16-22″) and weighs 10-15kg (25-35lb). The most typical coat colour is a bright foxy red but grey and dark brown individuals have also been recorded; all have conspicuous white and black facial markings. To the north of their range, in response to a cooler climate, longer-haired animals occur, some with distinctive spotted pelage.

J. Wolf & J. Smit. del. et lith.

M & N Hanhart imp.

FELIS TEMMINCKII.

Fishing Cat

Felis viverrina

T HE FISHING CAT has a discontinuous distribution through tropical and semi-tropical parts of Asia from Pakistan, northern India and Nepal through to Indo-China; also Sumatra, Java and Sri Lanka. They are to be found in marshy thickets, mangrove swamps and densely vegetated areas close to rivers and streams, preying on fish, wildfowl, frogs, crustaceans and molluscs, as well as snakes and small mammals. Fishing cats wade and swim readily and have been seen to catch fish by crouching on a rock or sandbank using their front paws as scoops. The forefeet are partially webbed with claws that are not fully retractable.

This is a medium-sized cat, with relatively short legs and tail and an elongated head. Head and body 570-850mm (22-33″); tail 200-320mm (8-12″); weight 5-8kg (10-20lb). The short coarse coat is generally a grizzled grey colour with dark brown spots and streaks arranged longitudinally. This species has the reputation of being aggressive and intractable in captivity.

J. Wolf del. J.Smit lith.

Hanhart imp

FELIS VIVERRINA

Margay
Felis wiedii

THE MARGAY resembles the ocelot in coloration but is smaller and has a proportionally longer tail. Head and body 450-700mm (18-28″), tail 350-500mm (14-20″). The eyes are strikingly large, the coat, short thick and plushy, and attractively marked. Skins were previously much in demand by furriers and traders.

The ocelot ranges from Mexico to northern Argentina, living mainly in forests but also in more open scrub country. It is an accomplished climber, preying on birds, squirrels, rats and oppossums.

There are several kinds of small spotted cat in the Americas. In Elliot's day the classification and relationships of the various species was very confused and establishing the identity of a particular specimen was not always easy. The latin name *F. tigrina* applied to this painting of margay cats actually belongs to the oncilla or tiger cat, another South American species, which is not depicted. The animal in the foreground does not belong here at all. This cat was based on a skin which was bought from a dealer and supposedly from the Americas. The specimen is still in the collections of the British Museum (Natural History), and has now been identified as an example of the Asian leopard cat *F. bengalensis*.

J.Wolf. &J.Smit.del.et.lith.

M&.N.Hanhart imp.

FELIS TIGRINA.

Jaguarundi
Felis yaguaroundi

THIS unusual-looking, slender, long-necked, short-legged South American feline has been likened by some to a weasel. The head and body length is 550-670mm (22-26"); the tail, which is extraordinarily long, 330-610mm (13-24"); and the weight, 5.5-10kg (11-22lb). The coat is short and coarse and occurs in two distinct colour phases: grey or dark brown to almost black, and a bright foxy red or chestnut. These two forms were once treated as distinct, but it is now known that they represent only variants of a single species and that kittens of different colours can even occur in the same litter.

The jaguarundi is found in lowland forests and scrubland from Arizona south to Argentina. It forages mainly on the ground but is also an agile climber feeding on birds as well as small mammals. Less nocturnal than most cats, it is usually seen singly or in pairs.

The illustration here shows the dark variant of the jaguarundi, the most commonly occurring form. The red or chestnut-coloured variant appears on the following page.

J.Wolf & J.Smit, del. et lith.

Hanhart imp.

FELIS JAGUARONDI.

Jaguarundi
Felis eyra

THIS is the jaguarandi in its red phase, when it is sometimes known as the eyra. A full description of this cat and its darker variant is on the previous page.

FELIS EYRA.

J.Wolf & J.Smit.del et lith.

M&N.Hanhart.imp.

Clouded Leopard
Neofelis nebulosa

THE CLOUDED LEOPARD, called in this illustration *Felis diardi*, is an inhabitant of the forests of South East Asia; in mountainous areas it can occur at elevations of up to 2,500m. It is a largely arboreal species feeding on birds and monkeys, as well as deer and wild pigs which are leapt on from overhead branches. Formerly found from Nepal through Indo-China to Malaya, Sumatra and Borneo, south-eastern mainland China and the islands of Hainan and Taiwan, it has disappeared from many parts of its range as a result of deforestation and hunting. Of all the cats, the clouded leopard probably has the most distinctive coat: grey or yellowish dramatically marked with large brown patches edged with black on the body with smaller rosettes and spots on the head and legs. The fur is short and coarse. This cat is quite large, approaching the common leopard in size, and usually has a particularly long thick tail, although animals from Taiwan are described as having a slightly shorter tail than other races. Head and body 610-1060mm (24-42″); tail 550-910mm (22-36″); weight 16-23kg (35-50lb). The animal depicted on the right of the painting has a short tail and probably represents the Taiwanese (Formosan) race *N.n.brachyurus*.

J.Wolf & J.Smit del.et lith.

M.& N.Hanhart imp.

FELIS DIARDI.

Lion

Panthera leo

THE LION once had a range which included northern India, the Middle East, and North Africa as well as the present distribution in the open country of Africa south of the Sahara. A tiny population of Asiatic lions still survive in the Gir Forest Sanctuary in Gujarat, north-west India, but they have disappeared from all other areas.

Lions are the only cats which are primarily social. They live in groups containing up to 30 individuals, known as prides, which are based on a number of closely related females and their young and one or more breeding males. The females do most of the hunting, preying off antelope, zebra and other large ungulates. Males grow larger than females, with head and body 1500-2500mm (5-8ft), tail 700-1000mm (3-3.5ft) and weight 150-250kg (350-550lb). Only males have the familiar mane, but while this is variable in size and colour the coat is invariably tawny, although occasional white lions have been recorded.

In the foreground of the painting are a lioness and two lions, one with a tawny mane the other black maned. In the background is a particularly heavily maned animal, a condition common to the North African and Cape races of lion, both of which are now extinct; its companion is not a lioness but a 'maneless' male lion. Two maneless lions became famous last century by preying on construction workers building the Uganda Railway in the region of Tsavo, and work was halted for several weeks before the animals were eventually killed. Despite such stories, however, lions do not usually attack human beings unless wounded or provoked.

FELIS. LEO.

J.Wolf & J.Smit, del. et lith.

M & N Hanhart imp.

Jaguar
Panthera onca

JAGUARS are the only New World representatives of the so-called big cats genus *Panthera*, similar in appearance to the leopard but more heavily built. The coat is short and commonly tawny yellow with dark brown or black spots, rosettes and large rings usually with some dots in the centre. Black individuals are not uncommon, particularly in forest habitats. Head and body 1120-1850mm (3.5-5.5ft); tail 450-750mm (1.5-2.5ft); weight 36-158kg (80-350lb).

Jaguars have been recorded from the south west United States, through Central America to central Argentina. They will adapt to semi-desert, scrub and marshland but are best suited to forest. Although they usually hunt on the ground they are excellent climbers, and indeed in some areas they live an arboreal life for part of the year while the forest floor is flooded. They are good swimmers and fish and cayman form part of their diet, which also includes large rodents such as agouti and capybara, and mammals such as peccaries and the tapir as depicted in the painting, where Wolf called it *Felis onca*.

FELIS ONCA.

J.Wolf & J.Smit del.&lith.

M & N Hanhart imp

Leopard
Panthera pardus

PROBABLY the most adaptable of all the big cats with a wide distribution across Africa, Asia and Asia Minor, leopards live in a range of habitats including rocky semi-desert and mountainous country as well as savanna and thick forest. In Africa they have even been recorded close to the suburbs of large towns. They are solitary and mainly nocturnal, preying on many medium-size mammal species such as monkeys, wild pigs, smaller antelope and deer, and are also partial to domestic dogs.

They are excellent climbers and will sometimes ambush their quarry from an overhead branch, often carrying quite large prey up into a tree to keep it away from scavengers. Leopards are smaller than lions and tigers, with head and body 910-1910mm (3-6ft), tail 580-1100mm (2-4.5ft), and weight 28-90kg (60-200lb). Animals from colder localities have long soft fur but most leopards are short haired and the commonest coloration is yellow or buff with a pattern of black rosettes and spots. Those from the tropics are generally darker and more heavily spotted. There are also completely black individuals, and these are sometimes referred to as black panthers but are not a separate species. In some parts of South East Asia more than half of the leopards in the population are black.

The illustration here (called by Wolf *Felis pardus*) shows Asian leopards with a crocodile. The individual in the background is a black panther, sometimes also called a melanic leopard, from the Greek *mēlas*, black.

Wolf & J.Smit del. et lith.

FELIS PARDUS.

M & N.Hanhart imp.

Leopard
Panthera pardus

Here again called by Wolf *Felis pardus*, as on the previous page, this plate shows a leopard with a baboon, and probably represents the North African race.

del. et lith.

M & N Hanhart imp.

FELIS PARDUS.

Tiger

Panthera tigris

THE TIGER once ranged widely across Asia from Siberia to the islands of Indonesia and west into Iran and the Caucasus, preferring areas of thick cover, reedbeds, forest and jungle. Several races are now thought to be extinct, notably those from Bali, Java and Iran, and others are rare and endangered. Tigers are solitary, nocturnal hunters, preying on wild pig, deer and other large ungulate species. The orange coat and dramatic striped pattern needs little description, but there is some variation, examples from Indonesia being smaller and darker while the Siberian tiger is considerably paler, thickly furred and larger in size. Head and body size 1400-2800mm (4.5-9ft); tail 600-950mm (2-3.5ft); weight from 100kg (220lb) for the Sumatran tiger to 300kg (670lb) for the Siberian race. Three races are depicted in the painting: asleep in the background is the small Sumatran form, in front is the familiar Indian or Bengal tiger, and seated the huge long-haired Siberian tiger, largest of all the cat family.

FELIS TIGRIS.

J. Wolf & J. Smit. del. et lith.   M. & N. Hanhart. imp.

Snow Leopard
Panthera uncia

THE SNOW LEOPARD is a high-altitude specialist living in the mountains of central Asia including the Tian Shan Mountains and the Himalayas, recorded at heights of up to 3,900m (13,000ft) but may go as high as 6,000m. It feeds on various mountain ungulate species such as wild sheep and goats, as well as marmots and pikas. Because of the loss of prey species to human hunters, snow leopards will prey on domestic stock and as a consequence are persecuted by herders and farmers. They are also hunted for their beautiful pelts, despite legal protection. Their fur is long and soft, grey or white in colour and marked with irregular black rings; the tail is particularly spectacular, thick and fluffy and very long. Head and body 1000-1300mm (3.5-4.5ft); tail 800-1000mm (2.5-3.5ft); weight 25-70kg (55-150lb).

FELIS UNCIA.

J Wolf & J Smit del et lith.

M & N Hanhart imp